Honouring My Wishes My Digital Life

Evelyn48

BLUEROSE PUBLISHERS
India | U.K.

For permissions requests or inquiries regarding this publication,
please contact:

BLUEROSE PUBLISHERS
www.BlueRoseONE.com
info@bluerosepublishers.com
+91 8882 898 898
+4407342408967

ISBN: 978-1-7399266-5-6

First Edition: December 2024

Evelyn 48

Honouring My Wishes My Digital Life

Evelyn48

Honouring My Wishes My Digital Life

Evelyn 48

Content

Content

Acknowledgement.

I would like to thank my family, loved ones and friends who helped me along the journey of developing the brand *Evelyn48* and *Honouring My Wishes My Digital Life*

I thank God for the inspiration placed upon me daily.

Thank you to my sister Patricia St. Hilaire and our cousin Sharon Forbes who both listened to me and repeatedly read and commented on numerous drafts.

Thank you, Satwinder Kundhi (NiQi), my design consultant from Print Inn

Thank you to Michael Francis, my partner who joined me on the journey of *Evelyn48* taking the time to understand my dream. Thank you for building relationships and creating interest in *Evelyn48* in the North of England while supporting me and developing the *Evelyn48* App.

To Deirdre Coward, my dearest friend from way back, who listened to me as we drove to and from our nights out, I say "Thank you."

Thank you, Abi Carter of African Caribbean Funeral Homes.

Thank you to Maxine Edgar of Bronze Ash Funerals.

Thank you to the focus groups for all the encouragement, thoughtful insights and suggestions.

Jackee Holder, Yinka Bandele, Mark Johnson, Sophia Powell, Maudlyn Aaron, Antonio Stewart

Thank you to my 5 mentors who joined my journey at different times and the procrastination clubs I paid to attend that held me accountable.

Last but not least, I thank my mother, Evelyn who lived at number 48. I set out to find a way to honour and remember my mum, at a granular level. Thank you Mummy xx

Introduction

Introduction

Honouring My Wishes, When I am Gone aims to bring a mature and methodical conclusion to your affairs. Thereby making the process seamless for your executors and a true reflection of how you want your passing to be concluded. This workbook works alongside your wishes as expressed in your Will.

2020 had unprecedented challenges for us all, one of those being how death is viewed, accepted, and prepared for. Death can knock at any time, being as specific as you can be about your wishes can help those you leave behind.

While thinking about death can be difficult, leaving your loved ones with clear instructions can prevent misinterpretations and ambiguity, giving those responsible for carrying out your final wishes the opportunity to fulfil them.

Honouring My Wishes When I am Gone will help to remove the guesswork, as you clearly set out your wishes.

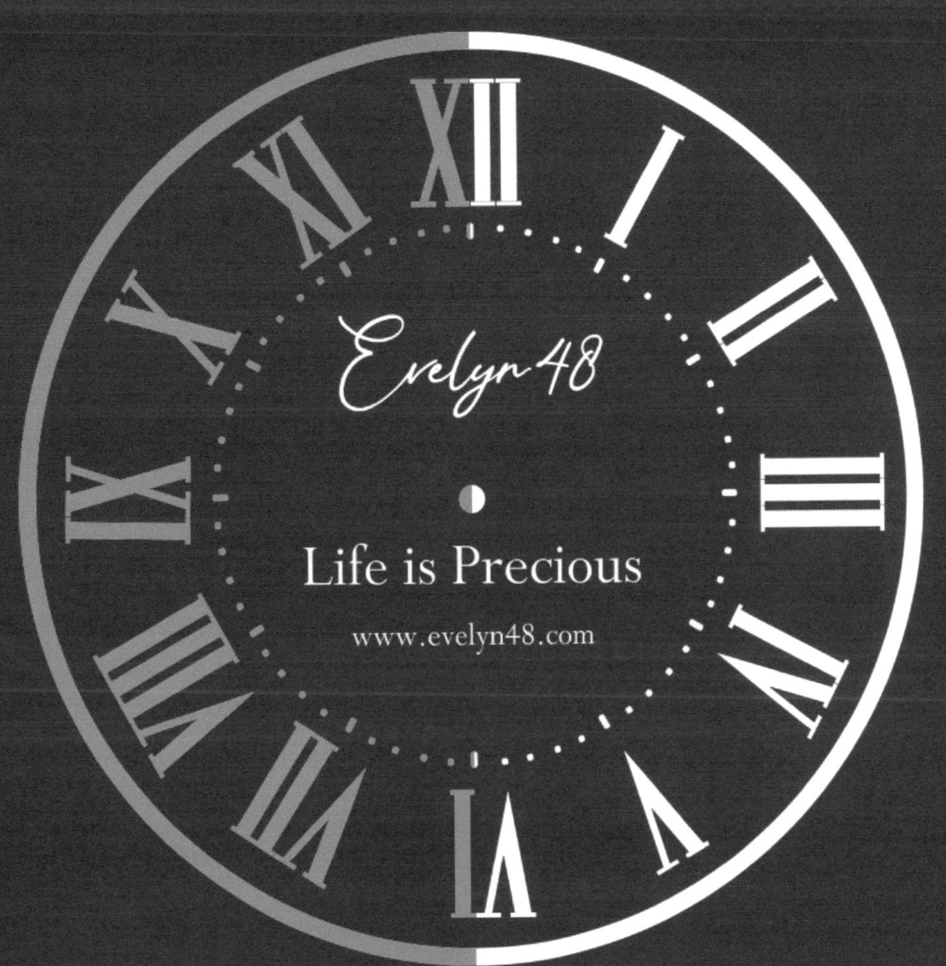
Evelyn 48
Life is Precious
www.evelyn48.com

Online Subscriptions

Online Subscriptions

WEBSITE:	
Username:	
Hard/Soft Copy:	
Password:	
Recovery Email:	
Cost:	
Paid From Account or With Credit Card	

WEBSITE:	
Username:	
Hard/Soft Copy:	
Password:	
Recovery Email:	
Cost:	
Paid From Account or With Credit Card	

WEBSITE:	
Username:	
Hard/Soft Copy:	
Password:	
Recovery Email:	
Cost:	
Paid From Account or With Credit Card	

WEBSITE:	
Username:	
Hard/Soft Copy:	
Password:	
Recovery Email:	
Cost:	
Paid From Account or With Credit Card	

Online Subscriptions

WEBSITE:	
Username:	
Hard/Soft Copy:	
Password:	
Recovery Email:	
Cost:	
Paid From Account or With Credit Card	

WEBSITE:	
Username:	
Hard/Soft Copy:	
Password:	
Recovery Email:	
Cost:	
Paid From Account or With Credit Card	

WEBSITE:	
Username:	
Hard/Soft Copy:	
Password:	
Recovery Email:	
Cost:	
Paid From Account or With Credit Card	

WEBSITE:	
Username:	
Hard/Soft Copy:	
Password:	
Recovery Email:	
Cost:	
Paid From Account or With Credit Card	

Online Subscriptions

WEBSITE:	
Username:	
Hard/Soft Copy:	
Password:	
Recovery Email:	
Cost:	
Paid From Account or With Credit Card	

WEBSITE:	
Username:	
Hard/Soft Copy:	
Password:	
Recovery Email:	
Cost:	
Paid From Account or With Credit Card	

WEBSITE:	
Username:	
Hard/Soft Copy:	
Password:	
Recovery Email:	
Cost:	
Paid From Account or With Credit Card	

WEBSITE:	
Username:	
Hard/Soft Copy:	
Password:	
Recovery Email:	
Cost:	
Paid From Account or With Credit Card	

Online Subscriptions

WEBSITE:	
Username:	
Hard/Soft Copy:	
Password:	
Recovery Email:	
Cost:	
Paid From Account or With Credit Card	

WEBSITE:	
Username:	
Hard/Soft Copy:	
Password:	
Recovery Email:	
Cost:	
Paid From Account or With Credit Card	

WEBSITE:	
Username:	
Hard/Soft Copy:	
Password:	
Recovery Email:	
Cost:	
Paid From Account or With Credit Card	

WEBSITE:	
Username:	
Hard/Soft Copy:	
Password:	
Recovery Email:	
Cost:	
Paid From Account or With Credit Card	

Online Subscriptions

WEBSITE:	
Username:	
Hard/Soft Copy:	
Password:	
Recovery Email:	
Cost:	
Paid From Account or With Credit Card	

WEBSITE:	
Username:	
Hard/Soft Copy:	
Password:	
Recovery Email:	
Cost:	
Paid From Account or With Credit Card	

WEBSITE:	
Username:	
Hard/Soft Copy:	
Password:	
Recovery Email:	
Cost:	
Paid From Account or With Credit Card	

WEBSITE:	
Username:	
Hard/Soft Copy:	
Password:	
Recovery Email:	
Cost:	
Paid From Account or With Credit Card	

Social Media Accounts

Social Media Accounts

WEBSITE:	
Username:	
Password:	
Recovery Email:	
Notes:	

WEBSITE:	
Username:	
Password:	
Recovery Email:	
Notes:	

WEBSITE:	
Username:	
Password:	
Recovery Email:	
Notes:	

WEBSITE:	
Username:	
Password:	
Recovery Email:	
Notes:	

WEBSITE:	
Username:	
Password:	
Recovery Email:	
Notes:	

WEBSITE:	
Username:	
Password:	
Recovery Email:	
Notes:	

Social Media Accounts

WEBSITE:	
Username:	
Password:	
Recovery Email:	
Notes:	

WEBSITE:	
Username:	
Password:	
Recovery Email:	
Notes:	

WEBSITE:	
Username:	
Password:	
Recovery Email:	
Notes:	

WEBSITE:	
Username:	
Password:	
Recovery Email:	
Notes:	

WEBSITE:	
Username:	
Password:	
Recovery Email:	
Notes:	

WEBSITE:	
Username:	
Password:	
Recovery Email:	
Notes:	

Web Accounts

Web Accounts

Please list all online accounts, such as PayPal, where there may be funds stored. It may be useful to advise your executors of any alternative names you go under such as on eBay, or email addresses.

Description of online account	*Login or access details*

Login and Password

Login and Password

WEBSITE:	
Username:	
Password:	
Recovery Email:	
Notes:	

WEBSITE:	
Username:	
Password:	
Recovery Email:	
Notes:	

WEBSITE:	
Username:	
Password:	
Recovery Email:	
Notes:	

WEBSITE:	
Username:	
Password:	
Recovery Email:	
Notes:	

WEBSITE:	
Username:	
Password:	
Recovery Email:	
Notes:	

WEBSITE:	
Username:	
Password:	
Recovery Email:	
Notes:	

Login and Password

WEBSITE:	
Username:	
Password:	
Recovery Email:	
Notes:	

WEBSITE:	
Username:	
Password:	
Recovery Email:	
Notes:	

WEBSITE:	
Username:	
Password:	
Recovery Email:	
Notes:	

WEBSITE:	
Username:	
Password:	
Recovery Email:	
Notes:	

WEBSITE:	
Username:	
Password:	
Recovery Email:	
Notes:	

WEBSITE:	
Username:	
Password:	
Recovery Email:	
Notes:	

Login and Password

WEBSITE:	
Username:	
Password:	
Recovery Email:	
Notes:	

WEBSITE:	
Username:	
Password:	
Recovery Email:	
Notes:	

WEBSITE:	
Username:	
Password:	
Recovery Email:	
Notes:	

WEBSITE:	
Username:	
Password:	
Recovery Email:	
Notes:	

WEBSITE:	
Username:	
Password:	
Recovery Email:	
Notes:	

WEBSITE:	
Username:	
Password:	
Recovery Email:	
Notes:	

Login and Password

WEBSITE:	
Username:	
Password:	
Recovery Email:	
Notes:	

WEBSITE:	
Username:	
Password:	
Recovery Email:	
Notes:	

WEBSITE:	
Username:	
Password:	
Recovery Email:	
Notes:	

WEBSITE:	
Username:	
Password:	
Recovery Email:	
Notes:	

WEBSITE:	
Username:	
Password:	
Recovery Email:	
Notes:	

WEBSITE:	
Username:	
Password:	
Recovery Email:	
Notes:	

Login and Password

WEBSITE:	
Username:	
Password:	
Recovery Email:	
Notes:	

WEBSITE:	
Username:	
Password:	
Recovery Email:	
Notes:	

WEBSITE:	
Username:	
Password:	
Recovery Email:	
Notes:	

WEBSITE:	
Username:	
Password:	
Recovery Email:	
Notes:	

WEBSITE:	
Username:	
Password:	
Recovery Email:	
Notes:	

WEBSITE:	
Username:	
Password:	
Recovery Email:	
Notes:	

Digital Photos

Digital Photos

WEBSITE:	
Username:	
Password:	
Recovery Email:	
Notes:	

WEBSITE:	
Username:	
Password:	
Recovery Email:	
Notes:	

WEBSITE:	
Username:	
Password:	
Recovery Email:	
Notes:	

WEBSITE:	
Username:	
Password:	
Recovery Email:	
Notes:	

WEBSITE:	
Username:	
Password:	
Recovery Email:	
Notes:	

WEBSITE:	
Username:	
Password:	
Recovery Email:	
Notes:	

Digital Photos

WEBSITE:	
Username:	
Password:	
Recovery Email:	
Notes:	

WEBSITE:	
Username:	
Password:	
Recovery Email:	
Notes:	

WEBSITE:	
Username:	
Password:	
Recovery Email:	
Notes:	

WEBSITE:	
Username:	
Password:	
Recovery Email:	
Notes:	

WEBSITE:	
Username:	
Password:	
Recovery Email:	
Notes:	

WEBSITE:	
Username:	
Password:	
Recovery Email:	
Notes:	

Online Journal

Online Journal

WEBSITE:	
Username:	
Password:	
Recovery Email:	
Notes:	

WEBSITE:	
Username:	
Password:	
Recovery Email:	
Notes:	

WEBSITE:	
Username:	
Password:	
Recovery Email:	
Notes:	

WEBSITE:	
Username:	
Password:	
Recovery Email:	
Notes:	

WEBSITE:	
Username:	
Password:	
Recovery Email:	
Notes:	

WEBSITE:	
Username:	
Password:	
Recovery Email:	
Notes:	

Online Journal

WEBSITE:	
Username:	
Password:	
Recovery Email:	
Notes:	

WEBSITE:	
Username:	
Password:	
Recovery Email:	
Notes:	

WEBSITE:	
Username:	
Password:	
Recovery Email:	
Notes:	

WEBSITE:	
Username:	
Password:	
Recovery Email:	
Notes:	

WEBSITE:	
Username:	
Password:	
Recovery Email:	
Notes:	

WEBSITE:	
Username:	
Password:	
Recovery Email:	
Notes:	

Cloud Storage

Cloud Storage

WEBSITE:	
Username:	
Password:	
Recovery Email:	
Notes:	

WEBSITE:	
Username:	
Password:	
Recovery Email:	
Notes:	

WEBSITE:	
Username:	
Password:	
Recovery Email:	
Notes:	

WEBSITE:	
Username:	
Password:	
Recovery Email:	
Notes:	

WEBSITE:	
Username:	
Password:	
Recovery Email:	
Notes:	

WEBSITE:	
Username:	
Password:	
Recovery Email:	
Notes:	

Cloud Storage

WEBSITE:	
Username:	
Password:	
Recovery Email:	
Notes:	

WEBSITE:	
Username:	
Password:	
Recovery Email:	
Notes:	

WEBSITE:	
Username:	
Password:	
Recovery Email:	
Notes:	

WEBSITE:	
Username:	
Password:	
Recovery Email:	
Notes:	

WEBSITE:	
Username:	
Password:	
Recovery Email:	
Notes:	

WEBSITE:	
Username:	
Password:	
Recovery Email:	
Notes:	

Additional Information

Additional Information

Additional Information

Additional Information

Additional Information

www.ingramcontent.com/pod-product-compliance
Lightning Source LLC
Chambersburg PA
CBHW040130180726
48295CB00005B/96

* 9 7 8 1 7 3 9 9 2 6 6 5 6 *